Black-eyed susans in Argyle State Park near Macomb

Acknowledgements

Unfortunately there is not room within these pages to thank each and every person whose assistance with this book was so invaluable. To the following organizations I extend my gratitude: Illinois Historic Preservation Agency, Illinois State Capitol Security, Illinois Tourism Office, Chicago Film Board, Chicago Board of Trade, Chicago Theater, Chicago Cubs, Bulls and Bears Sports Teams, The National Park Service, Shawnee National Forest, Crab Orchard National Wildlife Refuge, University of Illinois, Rendleman Orchards and Neighbor's Orchards. For showing me Chicago and sharing your homes with me special thanks to Mary Atols, John Hoffman, Linda Levy, and Sheila Arimond. (Keep feeding me that Häagen-Dazs coffee ice cream and I'll follow you anywhere, Sheila.) Thanks so much to those many Illini who shared tidbits of information, gave me directions, revealed their favorite places, and allowed me to stop for just an instant their lives and stories.

Although there is room for only one person behind the camera, the love, support, and encouragement of the following persons made me feel I was never alone: Melitta Wainio, B. Sterling Casselton, Jean Falk, Mary Beth Nevers, Shuby, Rita Plourde and Jim Holmen. Special thanks to Ginny Hostetter, Sheila, Melodee Monicken and Bill Gessner.

My greatest appreciation is for the infinite patience, understanding and love of my friend, lover, and spouse, JB.

Richard Hamilton Smith

Edited by James B. Patrick

Printed in Singapore

Designed by Donald G. Paulhus

ISBN 0-89909-155-5

Published by Foremost Publishers, Inc.
An affiliate of Yankee Publishing Inc.
Dublin, NH 03444

ILLINOIS
A Scenic Discovery

Photography by Richard Hamilton Smith
Introduction by Hal Higdon

Published by Foremost Publishers, Inc.

An affiliate of Yankee Publishing Inc.

Overleaf: Contour farming near Warren

The Heart of Illinois

A swift expressway connects Chicago with Peoria: four lanes of concrete aimed at the heart of Illinois. During four years when our daughter Laura attended Bradley University, my wife Rose and I frequently travelled that road. It took us nearly an hour heading west to clear the suburbs, row after row of dwellings, whose residents we never would know despite our many passages through their back yards. Only after we crossed the Des Plaines river in Joliet and turned south did farm houses finally outnumber tract houses.

Rose claimed that the next 90 minutes of our journey were suffered along the dullest road in America. Admittedly, expressway I-55 was almost painfully straight – and flat. We crossed a plain that the glaciers responsible for sculpting the lands north of Illinois somehow had failed to touch with their magic. Save for the characteristic Illinois cornfields, we could have been in western Kansas or eastern Colorado, where you sometimes scream for some variation in terrain.

Despite my wife's protests and my own eagerness for our drive to be done, I nevertheless found the monotony of the Illinois farmland comforting, as though it demonstrated a permanence all too often missing from our twentieth-century lives. That is why our regular journeys to Peoria – despite their monotony, maybe because of it – soothed me.

On those trips, a turn westward at Bloomington signalled an end to the straight and flat. Peoria lay a half hour ahead. Suddenly, we cut through a seam in the bluff above the Illinois river, and that city of 124,160 was below us on the other bank. The view as we descended the last mile into Peoria never failed to enthrall me, particularly at night, the city's lights glimmering over the water as though a miniature of Chicago's own skyline.

"Will it play in Peoria?" That was a rhetorical measuring rod political strategists used to assess their mentors' policies and positions. Some, including many Peorians, felt the statement demeaned their city as a "hick town." I disagreed, feeling it recognized Peoria as part of "real" America with overtones of heartland and hearth, and that if whatever *it* was that would not play in Peoria, *it* would not play anywhere of worth in this great nation of ours.

Still, Peoria is only one city, and certainly not the dominant one in Illinois. Rand McNally (itself headquartered in Illinois) lists 950 municipalities in the Road Atlas I use to guide us on journeys by automobile. Biggest, of course, is Chicago, listed at 3,005,072. Smallest listed, appropriately, is Middletown with 503 citizens.

I have never visited Middletown, which is 25 miles north of Springfield, the state capital, but in my journeys through Illinois, I have reached Cairo (pronounced "Cay-row"), located on the southernmost tip of Illinois at the juncture of the Ohio and Mississippi rivers and, for that reason, an important port city during the riverboat era. I stood at the point where those two rivers collided, watching millions of gallons a minute of fresh water rush past, able to stare into two other states: Kentucky to the south and Missouri to the west.

Farther north, the mighty Mississippi River also separates Illinois from Iowa to the west. The borders of Illinois with Wisconsin to the north and Indiana to the east are less easily discerned by the eye, unless you catch a road sign. The Illinois-Wisconsin border is but a line on a surveyor's map. The same is true about the Illinois-Indiana border roughly as far south as Terre Haute, at which point the Wabash River forms the divider.

But borders drawn on a map often fail to delineate a state or demonstrate how it is both different from and identical to its neighbors. During the year Richard Hamilton Smith drove through Illinois in his Jeep, taking the pictures that so magnificently grace this book, he felt at times he was photographing three states.

One was Chicago, central to the megalopolis that could be said to begin above Milwaukee in Wisconsin and stretch around the bottom of Lake Michigan through Gary and past the

Indiana Dunes, even up into Michigan. Depending upon where you draw your dotted lines, anywhere from three to ten million people live in this vibrant, urban area. (One might add to that the area of Illinois in the southwest attached to the St. Louis megalopolis.) Smith enjoyed his visits to Chicago, though he sometimes found it difficult to get the citizens of that city to slow down long enough to have their pictures taken. Harry Caray, the voice of the Chicago Cubs, nevertheless was among those who obliged Smith's lens.

Two was the large part of the arrowhead-shaped state down to about Carbondale, home of Southern Illinois University. The area outside of Chicago, for want of a better term, is sometimes referred to as "Downstate" – although the usually friendly people living within this area sometimes rightfully rumble: "Downstate of *what?*" Downstate includes the farmland that I crossed en route to Peoria, but it also embraces tourist towns like Galena in the north, and river towns like Quincy in the west, and college towns like Champaign (University of Illinois) in the center, towns that defy labeling, but nevertheless are pleasant places to live and raise children. (President Ronald Reagan was raised in one of them: Dixon, about 100 miles west of Chicago.) Smith often found himself pausing longer than he had planned in this second part of the state with its many visages so typically middle American.

Three was on the tip of the arrowhead. Draw a line east and west through Carbondale, and almost everything you see on the map below is green, part of the Shawnee National Forest. This area, with Cairo (population: 5,931) its dominant city, is oft referred to as "Little Egypt." Smith, understandably, had thought of Illinois as a northern state when he began his photographic odyssey, but here he encountered the South. Smith was surprised to find bald cypress trees. Compared to Chicago, life moved much more slowly, particularly during the steamy days of summer. Though farthest from his home, Smith found himself drawn to this area again and again.

I find myself similarly drawn to Illinois, though now residing just outside its borders in Indiana. Living on Lake Michigan, I can see Chicago's skyline on clear days. Three of the world's tallest buildings soar skyward from the horizon. I travel into their shadow frequently, passing over the high bridge on the Chicago Skyway that gives a broad view of the southern part of the city. (Alas, since there exists no scenic overlook atop the Skyway, you can't stop to enjoy that view).

The best view of the Chicago skyline is from the lake, floating offshore to the east, a popular pastime in a city where, despite numerous harbors in the parks, boatslips are at a premium. Best *time* for the view is at night, when the skyscrapers sparkle. Without a boat, you still can appreciate this spectacle by standing on the Olive Park or Adler Planetarium peninsulas that jut out into the lake. Lincoln Park, near the zoo, offers another sight angle, as do the various expressways – Kennedy on the north side, Eisenhower on the west side, and Dan Ryan on the south side. The first two were named after American presidents, the final after a local politician who controlled city services and thus had considerable clout.

"Clout" is an expression now recognized nationally, though coined in Chicago to describe "influence." The city offers other variations on the language. Most American cities merely have downtowns; Chicago has its "Loop," so named because elevated train tracks circle the central business district, thus loop around it. Few American cities can boast Chicago's varied architecture, from Louis Sullivan's textured facade on Carson Pirie Scott, the department store, to the glassy ponderousness of Helmut Jahn's new State of Illinois building.

Particularly during the mayorship of Richard J. Daley from 1955 to 1976, the world's best sculptors were persuaded that their careers would remain blighted, their artistic potential unfulfilled, unless one of their works adorned a Loop plaza. Best known is Picasso's lady across from City Hall, but Calder, Miro and Chagall also are represented. The Art Institute of Chicago has perhaps a greater collection of French impressionist paintings than you can find in any one museum in Paris. The Chicago Symphony Orchestra, under the direction of Sir George Solti, is recognized as the world's greatest. Chicago's sport teams are, well, less consistent, despite recent championship seasons by the Bears, during which the lions guarding the Art Institute were adorned with football helmets.

Bear running back Walter Payton, along with Mayor Daley, left an impact on the *city*, but license plates identify the *state* as "Land of Lincoln." Abraham Lincoln, born in 1809 in a log cabin in Kentucky, lived many years in Indiana, but spent his maturity in Illinois, arriving in 1830. His presence still dominates Springfield: Lincoln's home for 24 years, the office he shared with law partner William Herndon, the Old State Capitol in which he served in the Illinois General Assembly and delivered his "House Divided" speech presaging the Civil War, the Depot where he departed for Washington to become President, the tomb in which he was buried after his assassination in April 1865.

Wandering the steps of Lincoln's Tomb, Richard Hamilton Smith raised his camera in time to capture a small child touching the nose of the great President's statue. It is one of the many photographs following that capture the heart of Illinois.

Hal Higdon

Overleaf: Fall storm clouds and corn near Peotone

Fall farm aerial near Vermilionville

Soybean harvest near Tuscola

Canada geese, Horseshoe Lake Conservation Area

American lotus blossoms and cypress, Horseshoe Lake Conservation Area

Lincoln Home National Monument, Springfield

Lincoln's Tomb, Springfield

Millstone Bluff, Shawnee National Forest

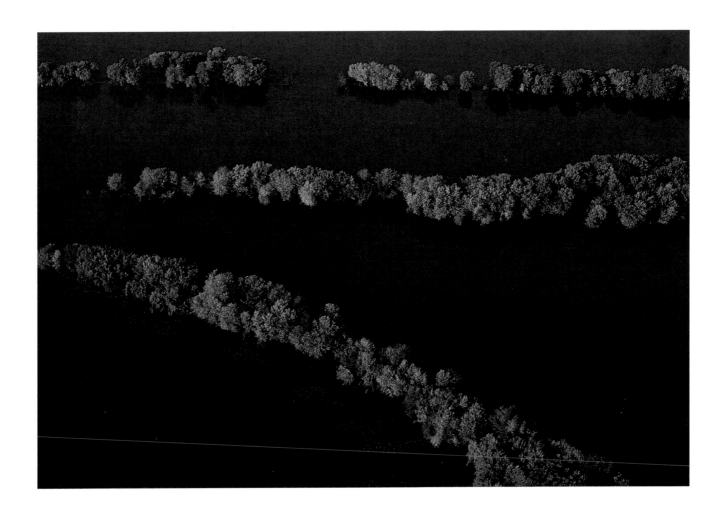

Mississippi River in fall flood near East Dubuque

Overleaf: Giant City State Park

Freeport farmer

Round bales and Holsteins, Jo Daviess County

"Winter sunbather" near Pearl

Quinsippi, historical pioneer village, Quincy

Fence at Carl Sandburg boyhood home in Galesburg

Carl Sandburg boyhood home in Galesburg

Twilight, Illinois State Capitol, Springfield

Interior view of dome, Illinois State Capitol, Springfield

Overleaf: Mississippi River sandbar, Big River Recreation Area

Male cardinal, Illinois state bird, near Elsah

Dawn over Stephenson County

33

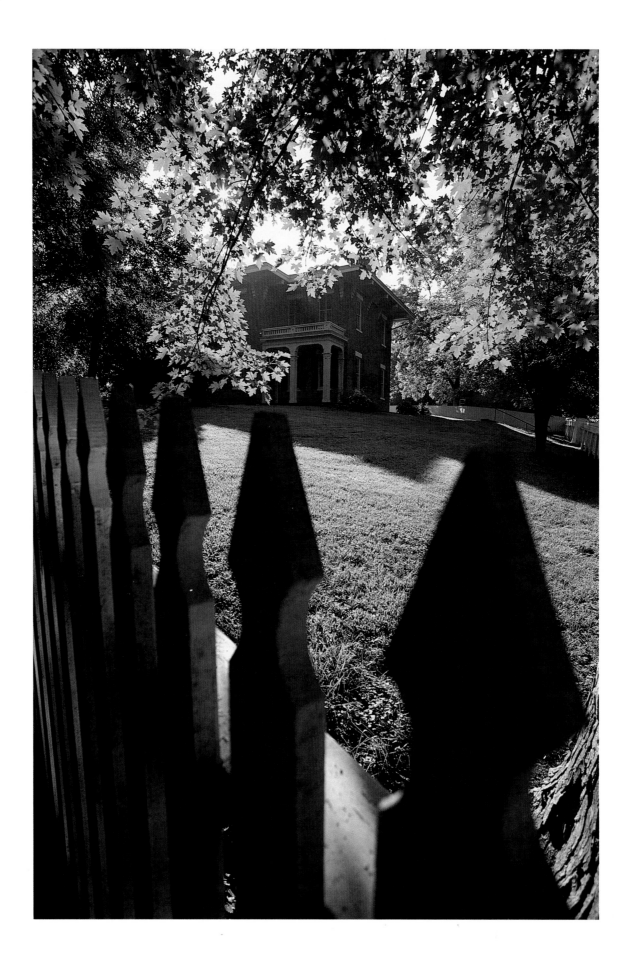

Ulysses Grant home in Galena

Civil War Memorial, Decatur

Full moon and deer in oaks near Apple River Canyon State Park

Church, Elsah

Aerial view of Old State Capitol in Springfield

Tabletop, Governor's Reception Room, Old State Capitol   *Overleaf:* Red cedar limbs and fall color, Mississippi Palisades State Park

New Salem State Park

New Salem State Park 'volunteer'

Creek in winter twilight, Sangamon County Conservation Area

Turkey gobbler, Shawnee National Forest

Earth sculpture and Illinois River fog, Buffalo Rock State Park

Dune patterns, Illinois Beach State Park   *Overleaf:* Aerial view, Chicago lakefront and Lake Michigan

Buckingham Fountain, Grant Park, Chicago

Seals at Lincoln Park Zoo, Chicago

Chicago Cubs baseball at Wrigley Field, Chicago

"Seventh inning stretch", Harry Caray, Cubs Baseball, Chicago

Chicago skyline from Olive Park

Untitled Picasso, Daley Plaza, Chicago

Chicago Bulls basketball, Chicago

Michigan Avenue bridge fresco and Wrigley Tower, Chicago

Historic Water Tower on Michigan Avenue in Chicago

Chicago traffic cop after a Cubs game   63

Illini football, Champaign-Urbana

Chicago Bears football, Soldier's Field, Chicago

Hepatica blossoms, Marshall County Conservation Area near Lacon

Aerial, Chicago's tallest buildings, John Hancock, Standard Oil, & Sears Tower   *Overleaf:* Pomona Natural Bridge, Shawnee National Forest

Cross country skiers, Rock Cut State Park

Ice floes on Illinois River, Pere Marquette State Park

Lincoln statue and State Capitol, Springfield

Street scene, Atwood

After the storm, Jo Daviess County   Draft horses in summer pasture near Berwick

Perch fishing, Crab Orchard Lake near Marion

Towboats on Ohio River near Cairo

Barn at sunset near Macomb

Whitetailed deer, Illinois state animal, Crab Orchard National Wildlife Refuge   *Overleaf:* Bluffs above the Great River Road near Elsah

Sunset, Wayne Fitzgerald State Park, Rend Lake   Lake Michigan sailing

Old Vandalia statehouse, Illinois' second statehouse

Statue of Stephen A. Douglas at Illinois State Capitol, Springfield

Mid-America personified!

Summer fun, White Pines Forest State Park

Aerial of Mississippi River islands near Blanding Landing

Seining the Mississippi River near Thebes   *Overleaf:* Violet, Illinois state flower, Springfield

Smooth phlox, Cave in the Rock State Park

Windsailing, Lake Springfield

94   Dogwood and statues, Lincoln's Tomb in Springfield

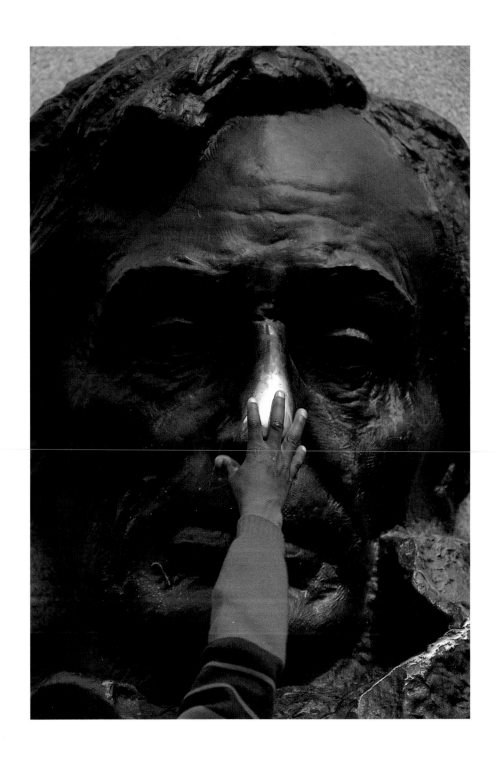

"Good luck rub", Lincoln bust at Lincoln's Tomb, Springfield

Redbud in rain, Eldon Hazlet State Park

Great blue heron in tupelo and cypress, Horseshoe Lake Conservation Area

Main street in Hillsboro

Wall mural, Warsaw   *Overleaf:* Young maples in grasses, Sugar River Forest Preserve

Beach at Royal Landing, Mississippi River, Calhoun County

Pasqueflower, Mississippi Palisades State Park

Nectarine harvest near Alto Pass   Peach harvest near Cobden

Hatchet toss, Aurora Rendezvous games, Aurora

Laona Heights Forest Preserve, Winnebago County   *Overleaf:* Garden of the Gods, Shawnee National Forest

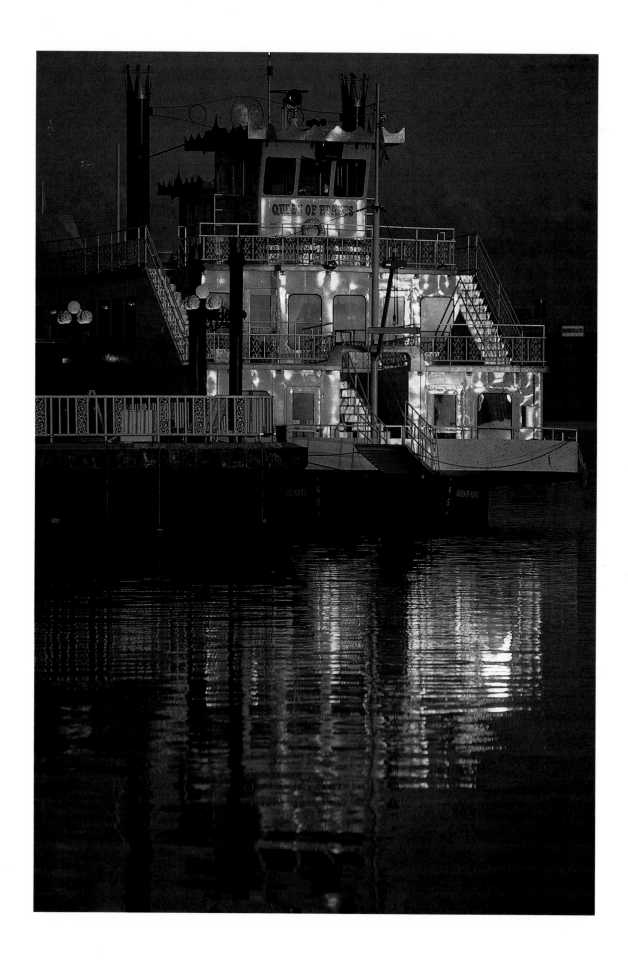

Riverboat, Quad Cities

Musician at Galesburg Railroad Days, Galesburg

Fourth of July parade, Downers Grove

Fourth of July parade, Downers Grove

Burden Falls, Shawnee National Forest

Bath time, near Harvard

Amish boys near Arthur

Horseshoe tracks in tar, Amish country near Arthur

Overleaf: Early snow, Jo Daviess County

Voyageurs in North canoe on Fox River, Aurora Rendezvous, Aurora

Old Market House in Galena

Little Grand Canyon, Shawnee National Forest   Bald cypress, Heron Pond Little Black Slough Nature Preserve near Vienna

Farmer and son watch corn harvest near Arthur

Twilight pig, near Time

Farm symmetry near Streator   Dogwood above lily pond near Etherton

White oak, Illinois state tree, and moon at dawn, Schuyler County